A Discovery Biography

JIM BRIDGER

— ◆ —

Man of the Mountains

by Willard and Celia Luce
illustrated by George I. Parrish

CHELSEA JUNIORS
A division of Chelsea House Publishers
New York ◆ Philadelphia

To Ray and Loretta, who may someday write their own
books

The Discovery Biographies have been prepared under the
educational supervision of Mary C. Austin, Ed.D.,
Reading Specialist and Professor of Education, Case
Western Reserve University.

Cover illustration: Janet Hamlin

First Chelsea House edition 1991

  3 5 7 9 8 6 4 2

ISBN   0-7910-1454-1

Contents

Jim Bridger:
Man of the Mountains

CHAPTER

1 Squirrel for Supper 7

2 Moving West 11

3 Jim's Big Adventure Begins . . 19

4 Fort Henry 24

5 Through South Pass 33

6 Discovery of Great Salt Lake . 41

7 Surprises 49

8 Two Arrows 57

9 Changes 65

10 Fort Bridger 70

11 The End of the Trail . `. . . 75

Chapter *1*

Squirrel for Supper

"Jim! Where are you, Jim?"

Eight-year-old Jim Bridger was aiming his gun at a squirrel on the fence rail. Slowly he squeezed the trigger. There was a loud bang.

Only then did he answer his little sister's calls.

When she reached him, Jim held up the three squirrels he had caught that morning. "Squirrel for supper," he announced proudly. "I'll skin them as soon as we get home. Maybe Ma will make you some gloves from the hides, after I tan them."

Jim's sister skipped with delight. Suddenly she remembered why she had come out looking for him. "If you don't hurry home, Ma will more than likely skin you. There are three carriages at the inn for you to clean. And there are all those horses to feed and water."

Jim frowned. He liked to hunt. He didn't mind too much working on the family farm. But he hated the thousand and one chores around the inn that his father and mother also owned.

"Why in tarnation do people have to stop this early in the day?" he asked.

He broke into a run, knowing he had a lot of hard work to do.

The year was 1812, and the place was Richmond, Virginia. Everyone seemed to be moving west, or wanted to. People talked about the new land there, rich land, cheap land. They even joked about how rich it was. They said you could plant seeds one minute. Then the next minute you had to jump out of the way because the seeds sprouted and grew so quickly.

People also talked about the wild animals. They told of huge herds of buffalo, elk, and deer. Thousands of beavers lived in the cool mountain streams just waiting to be trapped.

Whenever Jim Bridger heard these tales, he got a tingling of excitement down his spine. More than anything else, he loved to hunt and trap. He wanted to see the animals and places he had heard so much about.

To his surprise, Mr. Bridger had an announcement to make that very night. The Bridgers were gathered around the table, eating squirrel for supper. "Children," Mr. Bridger said, "your mother and I have decided to move west. We are selling our farm and inn here. We will be going as soon as we can get ready."

Young Jim Bridger let out a shout of joy. It might have been heard as far as the "Shining," or Rocky, Mountains.

Chapter *2*

Moving West

Mr. Bridger bought a covered wagon. All the family's possessions were loaded into it. Then they started west. There were five of them: Mr. and Mrs. Bridger, young Jim, his sister, and a baby brother.

Jim liked traveling. "Look at those bear tracks!" he shouted, pointing at the side of the trail.

"What bear tracks?" asked his sister. "You're always seeing things that no one else sees."

"Look out!" warned his father. "When you are driving, you are supposed to watch the road."

"Yes, sir." Jim pulled the team back onto the rough roadway. "But a bear went past here not long ago. I'll bet he's right back there in the woods."

Finally they came to the Ohio River.

Mr. Bridger sold the wagon and bought a flatboat. They loaded their belongings on the boat and continued their journey to St. Louis. Mr. Bridger bought a farm across the Mississippi River in Illinois.

The place where the Bridgers settled was called Six Mile Prairie.

The next few years were happy ones for young Jim. In winter he set out traps and sold the furs from the animals he caught. In summer he worked on the farm. He fished in the river and hunted in the woods. Sometimes he helped the ferrymen carry passengers, wagons, and animals across the wide Mississippi River.

During this time he grew tall and strong and self-reliant.

Then things changed. Mrs. Bridger became ill. Four years after coming to Six Mile Prairie, she died.

Mr. Bridger's sister came to care for the family. Soon after this, Jim's little brother died, then his father.

Young Jim Bridger sat with his head in his hands. He felt as if his whole world had come to an end.

He was no longer just a member of a family. He was now head of it. They needed money, and Jim was the only one to earn it.

"I know how to run a ferryboat," Jim said. "That's what I'll do."

Although he was not yet fourteen, Jim handled the ferry from Six Mile Prairie to St. Louis. He carried pigs, sheep, cattle, horses, wagons, and machinery.

The hours were long and the work was hard, even for a man. It took all Jim's strength to pole the ferry over the water. His muscles ached all night.

After a few months he had a chance to work in a blacksmith shop in St. Louis. Here men had iron shoes put on their horses. They had traps made and farm machinery fixed.

Learning to be a blacksmith was hard work, but Jim liked it. His boss, Phil Creamer, was a friendly man and a good teacher. Jim loved the sizzling sound the hot iron made when he pushed it down into a barrel of water. This made the iron hard. Jim also liked to listen to the people who came to the blacksmith shop.

Sometimes trappers came, who had been to the western mountains. They told of the beaver ponds and the thousands of beavers.

"How would you like to be a trapper, Jim?" one of them asked him. "There's money in beaver pelts. There's a big call for them now. Here and in Europe. They use the pelts for those tall hats so many men are wearing."

"There would be plenty of excitement, Jim," another trapper said. "Why, on one trip I saw grizzly bears as big as horses!"

"Yes," Jim Bridger thought, "it would be great to be a trapper." The money he would earn could send his little sister to school. Jim had never had time for school. He could neither read nor write. But he wanted his sister to have an education.

There was no trapping expedition starting out right then. But Jim was determined to join the next group heading west.

Chapter *3*

Jim's Big Adventure Begins

One day Jim Bridger rushed into the blacksmith shop waving a newspaper.

He spread the paper out on the bench and pointed to an advertisement. "Mr. Creamer!" he called. "Come here and read this to me! Please, won't you, Mr. Creamer?"

Phil Creamer rubbed his hands on his leather apron and leaned over the paper.

"Why sure, Jim." He read this ad from the Rocky Mountain Fur Company:

TO

Enterprising Young Men.
The subscriber wishes to engage ONE HUNDRED MEN, to ascend the river Missouri to its source, there to be employed for one, two or three years.—For particulars, enquire of Major Andrew Henry, near the Lead Mines, in the County of Washington, (who will ascend with, and command the party) or to the subscriber at St. Louis.

Wm. H. Ashley.

"Mr. Creamer, do you think they'd take me to trap beaver with them?"

Jim's blue-gray eyes were sparkling.

The blacksmith smiled. "Well, Jim, I reckon there's one way to find out."

"How, Mr. Creamer?"

"Ask General Ashley."

The ad asked for young men. Jim was young, only eighteen. He was almost six feet tall. Five years of blacksmithing had hardened his muscles.

At first, Ashley and Henry thought Jim was too young to be a trapper. But finally they decided to take him along.

On a spring day in 1822, the expedition was ready to leave. Jim's aunt and sister came to the landing to see him off. Phil Creamer and his family were there, too. It seemed to Jim Bridger that everyone in St. Louis was there to bid the expedition good-by.

One big keelboat was loaded with supplies and men. The other keelboat would follow in a few weeks.

Horses for the men to use were herded along the shore. Then Major Henry gave the command for the keelboat to move. Boatmen pushed on long poles. The people on the shore yelled and cheered. The men of the expedition shouted and fired their guns.

Jim Bridger looked back. There were his aunt and sister waving. They were all the family Jim had, and he was leaving them. There was Phil Creamer who had been like a father to him. He would probably not see them again for a long time. There was a stinging in Jim's eyes. He turned and looked upriver so no one would notice.

Chapter *4*

Fort Henry

Day after day the keelboat slowly crept up the Missouri River.

Jim Bridger spent most of his time on land. There he helped herd the horses. He shot rabbits and game for food. He explored the streams and prairies.

At last they came to the Indian village of the Arikaras.

That day the "Rees" were friendly. Jim and some of the others traded trinkets for buckskin jackets, shirts, and trousers. Along with Indian moccasins, these became the "uniform" of the mountain men.

On they went. The sun grew hotter. Jim wondered if they would ever reach the Rocky Mountains.

August came and a group of Assiniboine Indians rode up to join the trappers. They showed great signs of friendship. However, at the very first chance, they raced away with all the horses.

Jim never forgot this. From then on, he waited until he knew Indians well, before he trusted them.

Finally the expedition reached the mouth of the Yellowstone River, 1,800 miles from St. Louis. Major Henry said, "Here's where we'll build a fort."

Jim Bridger looked around him in disappointment. Along the river there were cottonwood and willow trees. Beyond, there was only the rolling prairie covered with sagebrush. Where were the Rocky Mountains he wanted to see?

Many men had already deserted the company because the work was too hard. Jim was the youngest man there, but he was used to hard work. As the trappers built cabins and a fort, he did his full share. It was only a small fort, but it gave them protection from storms, wild animals, and Indians.

As the weather grew colder, the men started trapping. The new men, or greenhorns, were paired off with experienced trappers.

Jim Bridger's partner showed him how to set beaver traps. They started out their first evening. Each man carried six five-pound traps, his rifle, powder, shot, and a skinning knife.

Young Jim groaned under the load. "Tarnation," he grumbled, "I feel more like a pack mule than a trapper."

They reached a small stream and followed it. A beaver had built a dam of sticks and mud across the stream. This had backed up the water into a small pond. The beaver's house, or lodge, was near the center. It was a round dome of sticks and mud.

"Now, Jim," the old trapper said, "you wade out there and set your trap the way I told you. Set it near the beaver's lodge."

Jim stepped into the icy water. Before he had waded a dozen steps, he was shivering. By the time he had set the trap, he was shaking from the cold. He wondered if he would ever get warm.

Early the next morning, Jim and his partner set out to check their traps.

Jim waded out into the pond. The old trapper built a small fire on the bank and waited there.

Jim reached the trap. He peered down through the still water. There, almost at his feet, was a drowned beaver. Jim Bridger was shaking from excitement now.

"Hey!" he yelled. "We've got one!"

As he leaned over and reached down for the beaver, he slipped on a mud-covered limb, hidden under water. Splash! Head-first, he plunged into the icy stream. Gasping and sputtering, he struggled upright. But, in his hands he held a full-grown beaver.

He tried to call out, but he was too cold and too excited and too wet.

"Now that's just fine, Jim," his partner said without any show of surprise. "You just bring him out here, and I'll show you how to skin him. Be sure to save his tail. Beaver tails are the best eating a man can get!"

Before Jim had a chance to get much more beaver fur, the second keelboat arrived at Fort Henry.

Major Henry sent for Jim Bridger.
"Jim," he said, "you've been a blacksmith. There's a blacksmith's outfit in
the boat. Get it ashore and set it up
in one of the cabins. Then you can
make metal hinges for our doors and
fix the traps and guns that are broken."

Jim nodded, in his serious-minded
way. He had come up the Missouri
River to be a trapper, not a blacksmith. But, if blacksmithing would help
the Rocky Mountain Fur Company, he
was willing to do it.

Chapter 5

Through South Pass

Jim Bridger spent the next winter in the Big Horn Basin of Wyoming. The Crow Indians there were friendly, and the trappers camped with them.

One day Jim was led to a large tepee. A fire burned in the center. Around the fire sat many chiefs of the Crow Nation. For some time they stared silently at Jim. He stared back, looking from one unsmiling face to another.

The fire threw strange shadows on the tepee. Jim licked his lips and swallowed hard. He wished someone would speak.

Finally Jim spoke up, "Even the wind talks more than the Crows."

"Yes," a chief nodded, "but the Crows want to make Jim Bridger a brother. The wind does not." With this, the chief smiled. The others smiled, too. All at once, everyone started to talk and laugh. Then the ceremony went on, and Jim was adopted into the Crow Tribe. His Crow name was *Casapy,* which meant "Chief of the Blankets."

By now Jim was almost twenty years old. His skin was tanned. His muscles had filled out, and he no longer looked so skinny.

Early the next spring, Jedediah Smith led a group of trappers from the Crow village. Jim Bridger was among them. They wanted to find a way to the Green River. It was on the other side of the Rocky Mountains.

They went southward and entered the Wind River country. As they climbed higher, the wind blew harder and harder. Jim Bridger pulled his beaver cap down over his ears. He clutched his buffalo robe and leaned into the wind. It was so strong he could hardly walk against it.

At last they reached more level country. There was very little shelter now. The icy wind screamed around them. They were too cold and tired to go any farther.

Jim Bridger pointed to a small thicket. He tried to yell, but the wind blew the sound away. Then he saw the others nod. All of them turned and staggered into the clump of trees. They huddled together to keep out of the wind as much as possible.

They tried to build a fire, but the wind was too strong. The men stayed in the thicket for two days without any food, without any fire, and without getting much sleep.

Once Tom Fitzpatrick poked Jim. "We'd better walk around a bit, Jim. We'll freeze to death if we don't." He had to yell to be heard above the wind.

The two of them staggered to their feet. Then they stumbled about in the darkness to get their blood circulating.

But after a short while, they crawled back into the thicket. Never in his life had Jim Bridger been so cold.

Then during the night, the wind died slowly down.

The trappers built a fire. Jim felt warmth creep back into his body. They cooked meat from a mountain sheep someone had shot. Jim Bridger ate his fill. Then he rolled in his buffalo robe and went to sleep.

The next morning they went on. Sometime near Jim Bridger's twentieth birthday, March 17, 1824, they crossed through South Pass.

Jim looked around him. To the north the tall peaks of the Rocky Mountains were jagged against the sky. To the south there were badlands.

"What a discovery!" he said to himself. "In the summer, wagons could go through here without much trouble." Jim was right. It was the easiest way through the mountains. Within twenty-five years, covered wagons by the hundreds would be rolling through South Pass.

Jim's eyes glowed as he looked west. Ahead were thousands of miles of unknown country. He picked up his rifle and moved forward.

Chapter **6**

Discovery of Great Salt Lake

Six months later Jim Bridger was with a group of trappers in northern Utah.

The trappers has just finished supper. The campfire was warm and the talk was low and easy. "You know," one of the men said, "I'd surely like to know where that crazy river goes." He nodded toward the Bear River flowing softly by the camp.

Some thought it went into the Green River. Others insisted it went north to the Snake River.

"Maybe it goes clear to the Pacific Ocean," said Jim.

The men argued. Jim decided to find out for himself.

The next morning he started to build a bullboat. He made the boat from willow limbs. He stretched fresh buffalo hides over the limbs and fastened them down. Then he sewed the hides together tightly. He melted some buffalo fat and poured it over the seams. This made the bullboat watertight.

It was not a beautiful boat. It looked like a big tub, and it was hard to handle. But it would take Jim Bridger where he wanted to go.

Into the bullboat went Jim's rifle, some powder, shot, and a supply of dried buffalo meat.

By now Jim Bridger wasn't quite so sure he wanted to go down an unknown river all by himself. But, no one else offered to go along. He stepped into the boat and pushed it away from the bank.

The trappers waved and yelled out their good-bys.

Jim waved back.

At first it was easy, riding the smooth water. After a while, he heard the voice of the river grow louder and stronger.

Jim thought of stopping and scouting ahead. Then it was too late. The rushing river sucked him into a canyon.

The rough water bounced and whirled the bullboat around. It smashed the boat against the huge boulders. Jim was sure it would be knocked to pieces.

Then, suddenly, the boat shot out of the canyon. Quickly Jim poled the boat ashore.

He climbed the steep canyon wall. The river ran to the southwest. In the distance he could see an open valley and mountains. Carefully he looked for Indian signs. There were no tepees, no smoke from campfires, no dust from traveling feet.

Still Jim was not satisfied. He climbed higher. At last he could see a long shimmer of silver. Jim decided it was a lake.

Then he went back to the bullboat.

He poled it down the Bear River. At last he came to the lake. The sun made him thirsty. He reached over the side of the boat and scooped up a handful of water.

As soon as he tasted the water, he spat it out. "Salty!" he roared, almost choking. "Tarnation! It's salt water! This must be the Pacific Ocean!"

He stared about him in amazement.

Before many days Jim rejoined his trapping brigade. Captain John Weber called out to him, "Well, Jim, have you been to the Pacific Ocean and back already?"

"I surely have," Jim announced. The trappers stared at him in disbelief. Then Jim held out his hand. "Here's a bag of salt to prove it."

The men crowded around. They stared at the salt. They tasted it.

Then one of them said, "I'll be a pollywog's uncle! It is salt!" A huge grin spread across his whiskered face. "Won't this taste good on beaver tails tonight! I'm getting mighty tired of using gunpowder for salt!"

A roar of approval went up from the other trappers.

In the summer of 1826 Jim Clyman and three of his fellow trappers sailed completely around Jim's "ocean." What Jim Bridger had discovered was not an arm of the Pacific Ocean. It was Great Salt Lake.

Chapter *7*

Surprises

After the long cold winter of trapping, Jim Bridger was glad to see spring come again. Now he could explore new country and find new beaver streams.

During the summer he and a small band of trappers set out to explore the area that is now known as Yellowstone National Park.

As Jim rode up to one of the geysers, it hissed steam. Jim's horse reared up.

"Whoa!" Jim Bridger yelled, pulling on the reins. "It's nothing but a puddle of hot water!"

The geyser hissed again. The water suddenly shot high into the air. Jim's horse turned and tried to run away. "Whoa!" Jim yelled again.

Jim stared at the geyser, hardly believing what he saw. "Tarnation," he whispered to himself. "No one will believe this when I tell them. Why, the water shoots up taller than a flag pole!"

When they came to the mud pots, Jim's horse tried to run away again. Jim listened to the plopping sound of the mud as it bubbled. He stared at the colors and scratched his head. "You reckon this is where the Indians get their war paint?" he asked a trapper.

"I'm not sure," the trapper answered. "I've been told the Indians are afraid to come here. They think it's evil spirits making all those noises."

Late in the year 1830, Jim Bridger and his trappers left Yellowstone to explore southward. Finally they came to the Bear River again and followed it down to Salt Lake Valley.

Here they spent a peaceful winter, trapping and hunting. Then one night in March, a band of Bannock Indians surprised them. The Indians raced away with all 80 of the trappers' horses.

For a while the trapper camp was in an uproar, then Tom Fitzpatrick took charge. "We'll get those horses back," he said. "We'll have to walk, but we'll get them."

"I'll go," said Jim Bridger. Other trappers stepped up, too.

"Take dried meat, a buffalo robe, and plenty of powder and shot," Fitzpatrick told the men.

In a short time 40 trappers started through the snow. All day they walked northward. And all night they shivered under their buffalo robes.

Five days later they found a large Bannock Indian camp. Close by were 200 to 300 horses, closely guarded.

"There they are!" Jim Bridger said.

Tom Fitzpatrick nodded. "Jim, you take half the men. Get as close as you can to the horses. I'll take the other men. When we charge the camp, you scare the horses. Run off as many as you can."

Quietly Jim led his men toward the horse herd. Where there was little sage-brush, they crawled on their hands and knees so they would not be seen.

At last there was no more cover between the trappers and the horses. Jim Bridger motioned his men to scatter out. Lying on his belly, Jim aimed his rifle at one of the Indians herding the horses. He took deep breaths to keep his hands from shaking.

Suddenly there came a crash of rifle fire from the Indian camp. Fitzpatrick's yell could be heard above the uproar.

Jim Bridger squeezed the trigger of his gun. Leaping to his feet, he yelled as loudly as he could. He raced at the horses. The trappers followed him, all yelling and waving their rifles.

The horse herd whirled about in confusion. Jim grabbed a pony's mane and swung himself onto the animal's back.

Other trappers mounted too.

They raced the horses to a safe place, then stopped to rest. All the trappers were there. No one was hurt.

"We came off with more horses than we lost," Jim Bridger grinned. "According to my count, there are about 120 ponies in this herd. Those extra 40 horses should pay us for our five days' walk."

Chapter *8*

Two Arrows

As the years went by, Jim Bridger found himself taking part in other Indian battles. In Indian country he always traveled carefully. He watched the ground for tracks. He watched the wild birds and animals. Whenever they were frightened, he tried to learn why.

One day Jim and a group of trappers met a band of Blackfeet Indians. The Indians waved a white flag.

Jim Bridger and Tom Fitzpatrick watched the Indians. All the trappers waited with their rifles ready.

"Looks like they want to powwow," Fitzpatrick said.

Jim nodded. "But they're Blackfeet. You can't trust Blackfeet." Jim turned to three trappers. "Go out and see what they want. We'll cover you."

The three trappers left their weapons and walked slowly toward the Indians. Three Indians came to meet them. The six men stopped to exchange greetings and smoke the peace pipe.

Suddenly the wife of a trapper rushed across the grass and threw her arms around an Indian brave. She was an Indian and this was her brother.

Excited talk came from the Blackfeet.

Jim Bridger rode forward. He sat tall and straight, his rifle across his knees. His eyes were narrow and his face stern as he watched the Indians for any sign of trickery.

A Blackfoot brave rode forward, too. He held an arrow in his bow, ready for trouble.

Chief Sun, the head of the tribe, moved up to the side of Jim's horse. Jim Bridger cocked his rifle. At the sound, the Chief reached out and grabbed Jim's rifle by the barrel. He tried to tear it from Jim's hand. The rifle exploded.

The bullet thudded harmlessly into the ground.

As his horse reared and twisted about, Jim heard the twang of a bow string.

Pain slashed his back like a burning knife. He grunted as he tried to hold onto the rifle and the horse.

Then another arrow hit his back. Suddenly his gun was ripped from his hands. The stock of the gun crashed against the side of his head. He was knocked from the saddle.

Almost as in a dream, he saw Chief Sun jump on his horse and ride away. Faintly he could hear the banging of rifles and the whir of arrows.

When the battle ended, Jim Bridger still lay where he had fallen with two arrows in his back.

"Jim," Tom Fitzpatrick said, "if I don't pull these arrows out, you'll go around the rest of your life looking like a porcupine. This is going to hurt."

Jim grunted, "Go ahead and pull."

Tom pulled, but the arrows wouldn't come out. "Here, Jim," said Fitzpatrick, pushing a piece of rawhide between Jim's teeth. "Bite down on this."

As Jim bit into the leather, Fitzpatrick pulled with all his might. Jim groaned through his clenched teeth. Suddenly the arrow came out.

Fitzpatrick went to work on the other arrow. He removed the shaft, but the arrowhead would not budge.

For three years Jim Bridger carried the three-inch arrowhead in his back. Then he met Dr. Marcus Whitman.

The trappers and Indians were gathered for their yearly rendezvous, or get-together, in the Green River Valley of Wyoming.

"Doctor," Jim said, "I have got an arrowhead stuck in my back. It gives me a lot of misery. You reckon you could cut it out?"

Dr. Whitman nodded and got his instruments ready.

Jim lay on the grass. Trappers and Indians crowded around to watch. They had no medicine to kill the pain.

"Are you ready, Jim?"

Jim nodded. "I reckon so."

Marcus Whitman took up his knife and started cutting. It took a long time, but at last the arrowhead came loose.

Now Jim was rid of the last of the two arrows.

Chapter *9*

Changes

Soon after this Jim Bridger married. His wife was the daughter of a Flathead chief. Her name was Cora.

"Have you ever been to the Yellowstone country?" Jim asked her. "Have you seen hot water shoot up in the air higher than that pine tree over there?"

Cora shook her head.

"Good!" Jim laughed with happiness. "We'll go there on our honeymoon."

When they started out, all Jim's trappers went along. Cora's father and some Flathead Indians went along, too.

"This is a heck of a honeymoon," Jim grumbled. "When you marry an Indian, you marry her whole tribe."

But he didn't really mind. Cora was a wonderful wife. She went with him and his brigade up and down the beaver streams. She took care of the tepee and mended all Jim's clothes. Most important, she made him happy. His joy was complete when their daughter, Mary Ann, was born.

But things were not going well in the fur trade. Tall silk hats were replacing those made from beaver hides. The price of beaver furs went down. There were few beavers left to trap.

Many of the mountain men were
leaving the mountains. "Better come
with us, Jim. The time of the fur trade
is over."

But Jim Bridger stubbornly shook his
head. "Not for me," he said.

But his old trapping partners were
right. The days of the fur trade were
coming to an end.

Other things, however, were happening
in the Rocky Mountains. Dr. Marcus
Whitman and his family had gone on
to settle in Oregon. Each year a few
more wagon trains made the trip over
the mountains, on their way to Oregon
or to California.

One day Jim saw his first big wagon
train. Guiding the train was his old
pal, Tom Fitzpatrick.

The two trappers hugged each other and danced around like a pair of youngsters on the last day of school.

Before the wagon train moved on, Jim asked Tom if he would take six-year-old Mary Ann to Marcus and Narcissa Whitman in Oregon. "Tom," he said, "I want Mary Ann to have book-learning. Marcus said he would teach her when she got old enough."

When the wagon train pulled out, little Mary Ann Bridger stood in the back of a wagon. Tears rolled down her cheeks as she waved good-by.

Jim hated to see her go. But he knew times were changing. Book-learning was becoming more important. He wanted Mary Ann to have the schooling he had missed.

Chapter *10*

Fort Bridger

The following summer Jim saw more and more wagon trains creaking across the plains. The Indians saw them, too, and became more warlike. They didn't want to lose their hunting grounds to the white men.

But Jim knew the settlers would keep on coming. They would need supplies and a place to repair their wagons. In 1843 Jim decided to start such a place in Wyoming.

At first, Fort Bridger was only a trading post with a blacksmith shop and sheds for the animals. Later several log buildings were surrounded by a high picket fence to make it a fort.

It became an important way station for the pioneers traveling westward. Here they could trade for strong horses and oxen. They could hire guides or get information about the trails to Utah or California or Oregon. Fort Bridger made the trip easier for thousands of pioneers.

But it was not to be a happy place for Jim. Three years after the fort was built, his wife, Cora, died.

Other tragedy soon followed.

In March 1848, the snow was deep and the wind sharp and cold. Three

men staggered into the fort, more dead than alive. Jim was surprised to see an old friend, Joe Meek.

Joe had married an Indian woman and had moved to Oregon.

"There's been Indian trouble up our way, Jim," he said. "Bad trouble. The Cayuse Indians went on the warpath. They burned the Whitman Mission. They killed Marcus and his wife." Joe Meek stopped. Jim Bridger sat in stunned silence.

At last Jim asked, "What about my Mary Ann, Joe?"

"I really don't know, Jim. They say she was carried off by the Indians."

Somehow Jim knew he would never see Mary Ann again. Later he learned that she was dead.

In time, Jim took another wife, a Ute Indian. When their child, Virginia, was born, the mother died.

While still at Fort Bridger, Jim married a third time. His last wife was named Little Faun. She was a lovely Shoshone princess.

Ever since Mary Ann's death, Jim had worried about the safety of his family. "Could you be happy among white people?" he asked Little Faun.

She smiled. "I can be happy anywhere."

"I'd like to get a farm in Missouri. There you can be safe, and Virginia can go to school."

So Jim moved his family to Missouri and tried to settle down.

Chapter *11*

The End of the Trail

Jim Bridger was not happy away from the mountains. Soon he returned to them.

He spent many of his last years guiding wagon trains and the United States Army. The Army was sent to survey the land and also to protect the settlers from Indian attacks.

Jim took good care of the groups he guided. He knew the Indians and how to go through their country.

While building Fort Phil Kearney, the army needed supplies from another fort, Fort Reno. Captain Burrows was sent to get them. Jim Bridger went along as guide and scout to the captain.

Along the trail that day, Jim found many buffalo skulls. On the bleached white bones were strange markings. They showed an arrow, a broken gun, and a woman with a zigzag line around her face.

These were signs of trouble up ahead. Bad trouble.

When Captain Burrows gave orders to camp, Jim Bridger said, "I believe we'd better go on, Captain."

"Go on!" the officer shouted. Then he looked at Jim's serious face. "Why do you say that, Jim?"

"There's going to be a fight on Crazy Woman Creek. The buffalo skulls tell all the Sioux to be there."

Captain Burrows looked at his 200 tired men. "You're sure, Jim?"

Jim Bridger nodded.

Captain Burrows still seemed doubtful. Then he roared, "Prepare to march! We will camp at Crazy Woman Creek tonight!"

Unhappy and grumbling, the tired men fell into line again.

At last they reached Crazy Woman Creek. Here they found 26 men who had been on their way to Fort Phil Kearney. Several hundred Sioux had

attacked them from the surrounding hills. The arrival of Captain Burrows and his men sent the Indians fleeing and saved 26 lives.

In 1868 Jim Bridger left the army. He went to his farm in Missouri. Here he lived with his daughter, Virginia.

Jim was old now. His health was beginning to fail. He also found out that he was going blind.

But there were happy moments for Jim Bridger. The children who lived nearby discovered that Jim was a wonderful storyteller. They sat breath-less as he told of the trappers and the Indians. They roared with laughter at his tall tales.

On July 17, 1881, when he was 77 years old, Jim Bridger died.

He had lived the life he loved, the life of a mountain man. He had discovered Great Salt Lake and had explored large areas of the West. He had been a great trapper and a brave army guide.

He is still remembered for his courage and his loyalty to his fellow trappers. Jim Bridger will always be known as a king of the mountain men.